FRANCIS
NGANNOU

Francis Ngannou punches Ciryl Gane in their heavyweight championship fight.

FRANCIS NGANNOU

ODYSSEYS

ÁLVARO MICHAEL

CREATIVE EDUCATION · CREATIVE PAPERBACKS

Published by Creative Education and Creative Paperbacks
P.O. Box 227, Mankato, Minnesota 56002
Creative Education and Creative Paperbacks
are imprints of The Creative Company
www.thecreativecompany.us

Copyright © 2025 Creative Education, Creative Paperbacks
International copyright reserved in all countries.
No part of this book may be reproduced in any form
without written permission from the publisher.

Design by Graham Morgan
Art direction by Tom Morgan
Edited by Kremena Spengler

Images by Alamy Stock Photo/Slavko Midzor/PIXSELL, cover, 6; Getty Images/ANDREAS SOLARO, 29, Brandon Magnus, 39, Chris Unger, 2, 56, 75, DANIEL BELOUMOU OLOMO, 52, 62, 70-71, FRANCK FIFE, 30, 34, Jeff Bottari, 8, Josh Hedges, 44, 48-49, Justin Setterfield, 60, Mike Roach, 12; Shutterstock/LightField Studios, 20; Unsplash/Earth, 33, Edouard TAMBA, 26, Sylwester Walczak, 65; Wikimedia Commons/Airman 1st Class Kerelin Molina, 4-5, Andrius Petrucenia, 11, BillCramer, 19, Jguk 2, 69, Minette Lontsie, 24, Prosper Mekem, 14

Library of Congress Cataloging-in-Publication Data
Names: Michael, Álvaro, author.
Title: Francis Ngannou / by Álvaro Michael.
Description: Mankato, Minnesota : Creative Education and Creative Paperbacks, [2025] | Series: Odysseys in extreme sports | ATOS 6.5 | Includes bibliographical references and index. | Audience: Ages 12-15 years | Audience: Grades 7-9 | Summary: "Step into the Octagon with mixed martial arts (MMA) fighter Francis Ngannou. Witness triumphs, challenges, and risks in this extreme sports title for high school readers. Includes action photos, a glossary, index, and further resources"– Provided by publisher.
Identifiers: LCCN 2024025240 (print) | LCCN 2024025241 (ebook) | ISBN 9798889893141 (lib. bdg.) | ISBN 9781682776803 (paperback) | ISBN 9798889894254 (ebook)
Subjects: LCSH: Ngannou, Francis, 1986—Juvenile literature. | Mixed martial arts-Cameroon-Biography-Juvenile literature. | Ultimate Fighting Championship (Organization)-Juvenile literature. | Immigrants-Civil rights-Juvenile literature.
Classification: LCC GV1113.N44 A57 2025 (print) | LCC GV1113.N44 (ebook) | DDC 796.81092 [B]-dc23/eng/20240711
LC record available at https://lccn.loc.gov/2024025240
LC ebook record available at https://lccn.loc.gov/2024025241

Printed in China

Ngannou wanted to be a boxer before taking up mixed martial arts (MMA).

Francis Ngannou at UFC Fight Night 86 in Zagreb, Croatia

CONTENTS

Introduction **9**

Cameroon to Paris **15**

Father's Footsteps? 20

Learning MMA **31**

'American Boy' 39

Ngannou vs. UFC **42**

'He's the Man' 49

Reflections **63**

The Francis Ngannou Foundation 71

Selected Bibliography **76**

Glossary **77**

Websites **79**

Index **80**

Introduction

Francis Ngannou has beaten the odds again and again. In search of an opportunity to fight professionally, he traveled thousands of miles, largely on foot, from his home in Cameroon to Europe.

OPPOSITE: Francis Ngannou battles Stipe Miocic in their heavyweight championship fight at UFC 260 on March 27, 2021, in Las Vegas, Nevada.

The 6-foot-4 athlete didn't even learn what mixed martial arts (MMA) were until he was 27. However, within just a couple of years of starting the sport, he signed with the Ultimate Fighting Championship (UFC) and became known for having one of the strongest punches ever recorded. He repeatedly knocked out his opponents in just one or two rounds, and for two years he reigned as UFC **heavyweight** champion.

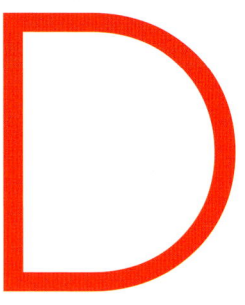espite his enormous size, Ngannou is a polite, calm, and inward-looking athlete, devoted to his

A UFC championship belt

OPPOSITE Francis Ngannou poses for a portrait after his victory at UFC 270 on January 22, 2022, in Anaheim, California.

family and to Cameroon. He is also an example of quiet determination, beginning life in poverty and growing into an internationally famous fighter. And while MMA and boxing are his passions today, the path that led him there would have been impossible had he not had the courage to dream.

FRANCIS NGANNOU

Cameroon to Paris

Ngannou was born on September 5, 1986, in the small village of Batié, Cameroon, Africa. He was the second of five children of Emmanuel Fosso and Kamegni Christine.

OPPOSITE: A view of Batié, Cameroon, where Francis Ngannou was born

When Ngannou was just a few years old, his mother had already noted that he was larger and stronger than other youngsters his age. "Even when he would draw water," she recalls, "at five years old he carried the containers of a ten-year-old child. The wood he collected was always the big bundles."

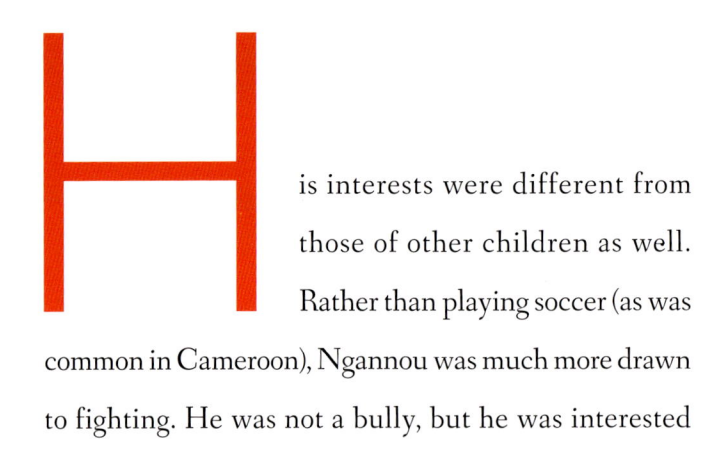

His interests were different from those of other children as well. Rather than playing soccer (as was common in Cameroon), Ngannou was much more drawn to fighting. He was not a bully, but he was interested in fighting as a sport. "He would fight with the banana trees out in the bush," says his mother. He obsessed over boxing movies, even though he was forbidden from watching them. He also talked incessantly about famous boxer Mike Tyson—despite never having seen him actually fight. The desire to become a professional fighter developed early in Ngannou's life.

However, to attain a dream like that was not easy in Batié, and any sort of fighting career was far down the road, if not impossible. His childhood was full of poverty, hunger, and frustration. His father was a known street fighter who repeatedly got in trouble with the law, and he often hit his children and wife. When Ngannou was six years old, his parents divorced, and his father left the family. Ngannou was sent to live with his aunt and cousins for a couple of years. He spent the rest of his youth moving from the household of one relative to another. Although his mother would remain an important part of his life, there were long periods of time when he didn't see her.

As he grew up, Ngannou became known in his village for his dream of being a fighter. It was an unusual desire, and people often tried to dissuade him from pursuing it. To them, a boy should follow in his family's footsteps and grow up to be a farmer, a mechanic, a carpenter—not a boxer.

Mike Tyson was one of Ngannou's idols.

Father's Footsteps?

At an early age, Ngannou became acquainted with a deep sense of shame for his father. When people would learn that he was the son of Emmanuel Fosso, known in the community as a street fighter, they tended to react with disapproval. They would see Ngannou and his size and strength, and they would tell him he'd probably end up like his father: violent. However, Ngannou wanted a reputation that was better than his father's. Though he wanted to fight, he didn't want to be known as a violent person. It is a lesson that he says has guided him for his whole life. He reserves fighting only for the fighting ring.

Indeed, the members of his village were mostly poor, including Ngannou's family. "The people there are very hopeless," says Ngannou, recalling his childhood, "because they feel like nothing is made for them. They feel like they are forgotten." People were aware that their possibilities in life were limited, and they accepted it. Thus, they didn't know what to make of this boy whose ambition was to be the world's greatest boxer.

Life at school was difficult for Ngannou. His middle school was six miles (10 km) away from home, and he had to

"WHEN NGANNOU WAS JUST NINE OR TEN YEARS OLD, HE STARTED WORKING IN THE SAND MINES OF BATIÉ."

walk two hours to get there. That meant waking up at 5 a.m. just so he could arrive on time. There was often no food for breakfast, and he went hungry during the day. Sometimes he would leave school early just so he could get home and eat. In addition, school in Cameroon was not free. Frequently his family couldn't afford school payments, and whenever that happened, Ngannou was sent away by his teachers.

When Ngannou was just nine or ten years old, he started working in the sand mines of Batié with his brother to help support his family, shoveling sand into trucks. He only made $1.90 a day. "We had no choice," Ngannou recalls. "We needed to survive." Money was needed at home for food, oil, and schoolbooks.

Other children were not working at that age, and the shovel alone was heavy in his hands. "But lucky for me, I was bigger than nine years old, so I could carry it, and I was strong." During the summer wet season, he often had to work in the rain. He and his

Workers at a sand mine in Africa

brother would get cold, and they shoveled harder to stay warm. He despised the work. In all, Ngannou spent more than ten years at the sand mines.

At 22, Ngannou resolved to study boxing in Douala, Cameroon's largest city. However, he was a fast learner, and after some years of boxing in Douala, there was nothing left for him to learn. He started to think about finding opportunity elsewhere, beyond Douala, beyond Cameroon. In addition, he had become concerned that, if something ever happened to his mother,

he would not be able to afford to take care of her. He decided that, if he wanted to master professional fighting and provide a greater income to his family, he would leave Cameroon to pursue boxing in Europe. Thus, on April 3, 2012, Ngannou took his first steps north. Three thousand miles lay ahead of him.

From Cameroon, Ngannou passed through Nigeria, Niger, and Algeria. In each of these African countries, he met difficult challenges: thirst, hunger, police, desert heat. After many weeks, he reached Morocco. Over the next year, he hid in a Moroccan forest with other migrants while making many attempts to cross into Europe.

Between attempts, he kept up his fitness regimen, doing push-ups and ab workouts on the forest floor. Sometimes he would find an Internet café where he would watch videos of Mike Tyson, his inspiration.

Finally, on April 3, 2013, exactly one year after leaving Cameroon, he succeeded in crossing on an inflatable raft with nine other migrants. They were rescued by a Spanish Red Cross vessel. In Spain, he was sent to a detention center for two months for illegal entry. He continued to do push-ups in his prison cell. He did not know what his fate would be and whether he would be sent back. Fortunately, because Spain and Cameroon do not have a repatriation agreement, Ngannou was allowed to stay.

Migrants receive life jackets during a rescue off the coast of Africa.

FRANCIS NGANNOU

Learning MMA

Ngannou had heard that the United Kingdom had a good boxing reputation. However, because the U.K. no longer had open borders with the rest of Europe, he would have had to cross more difficult hurdles to get there. By this point he was tired from his long journey, and he hoped to start boxing as soon as possible.

OPPOSITE: Francis Ngannou trains at the MMA Factory gym in Paris, France, on April 21, 2017.

Initially he thought of traveling to Germany. However, when he reached Paris, France, it was late, and he needed a place to rest. A fellow Cameroonian man showed Ngannou an underground parking lot where he was sleeping. Ngannou found some boxes and laid them on the floor as a mattress. That night, he decided not to continue on to Germany after all—he would make his start in France.

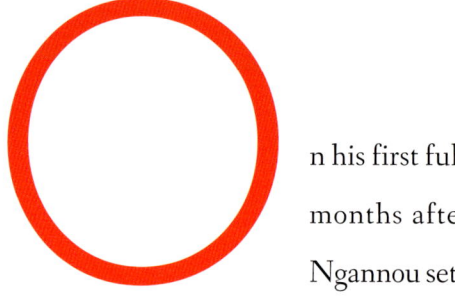n his first full day in Paris, 14 months after leaving Batié, Ngannou set out to find some-

Ngannou started his journey in competitive fighting in Paris.

Francis Ngannou trains at the MMA Factory gym in Paris.

where to box. He asked strangers on the street if they knew of any good boxing gyms, and in the afternoon he found one. He walked in and asked the front-desk receptionist if he could speak with the coach. She said that the coach wasn't there but that Ngannou could meet with one of the class instructors, Didier Carmont.

gannou told Carmont his story and how he wanted a place to train. Carmont responded with compassion and talked on Ngannou's behalf with the gym's coach, who permitted Ngannou to use the gym

and attend trainings at no cost. Carmont gave him 50 euro ($55), which Ngannou used to buy a T-shirt, a pair of shorts, a bag, and a towel. From that point on, Ngannou attended the gym regularly, and the coach saw that Ngannou was a very good boxer.

Just a couple of weeks after Ngannou began training, Carmont suggested that Ngannou might want to pursue MMA, which would give him better opportunities to make money than boxing. Ngannou was unfamiliar with the sport. Carmont explained that MMA involves a mix of wrestling, grappling, jiu-jitsu, striking, and other techniques. In addition, he believed Ngannou had the potential to become a UFC champion. However, Ngannou did not express interest. His preference was boxing.

After only a few weeks, the fighting gym closed down for a month's vacation. During that time, Ngannou discovered another gym called MMA Factory, one of France's largest MMA gyms. There, he met the coach, Fernand López. Like Ngannou, López was from Cameroon, and he had been on the French MMA scene from 2006 to 2010. When he heard Ngannou's story, López welcomed him into the gym and allowed him to sleep there as well.

Soon after Ngannou began training with him, López said (just like Didier Carmont had) that MMA could be a good route for Ngannou. The boxing world was rather closed—a boxer needed to know the right people if they wanted to advance. In contrast, it was much easier to enter MMA fighting, and there was plenty of prize money to be won.

This time, Ngannou agreed to try it, and he began taking MMA classes with López in addition to boxing. Thus Ngannou's career in MMA was set in motion, although he did not know it yet. He was soon surprised that MMA was fun! Not only that, but López noticed how Ngannou was an incredibly quick learner—he was capable of picking up the concepts of MMA much faster than other students.

While Ngannou studied MMA with López, Didier Carmont continued to help him out. Carmont started to pay for Ngannou's membership at MMA Factory, and he gave Ngannou a small apartment for two months rent-free.

Just a month after Ngannou started his MMA training, López signed Ngannou up for official fights. His first fight

'American Boy'

Since childhood, Ngannou had seen himself fighting in the United States and even requested that his siblings call him "American Boy." He would also make people call him "San Francisco," like the city in California. In fact, when he learned to write his signature at age ten, he made his signature "SF" and to this day still signs his name that way. Ngannou still remembers the sheer joy and disbelief he felt when he arrived in the United States for the first time. He was driven by a chauffeur to the Hyatt Regency. He had never seen a hotel so big. From his hotel room, he called his parents back in Cameroon. "I've made it!" he told them. "I've made it to America."

was in November 2013 against Rachid Benzina. In less than two minutes, Ngannou succeeded in getting on top of Benzina and performing a **shoulder lock**. Benzina **tapped out**, and as a result, Ngannou won by **submission** in the first round. With that win, Ngannou realized he was naturally adept at MMA, even if boxing was still his greatest passion.

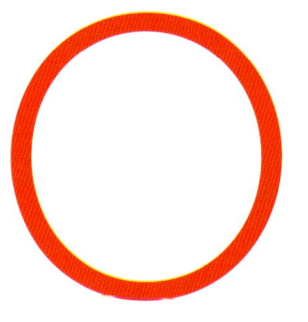

Over the next year and a half, Ngannou won more MMA fights, in France, Switzerland, and Bahrain. Out of six fights, he lost only one. He was thrilled about the cash prizes he received from his wins—

his first prize was 2,000 euro ($2,100)! He started sending money home to his family. In France, Ngannou gained a reputation as an **ominous** fighter, and it became difficult to find opponents who would accept matches with him.

The next major step in his MMA career occurred on his 29th birthday. Ngannou received a call from his coach, López, who informed Ngannou that he had just gotten him a contract with the UFC! If Ngannou signed, his next fight would be in four months.

It was astonishing news. Although Ngannou still wanted to pursue boxing, he saw the potential of a career with the UFC. He realized it would give him more fights, more attention, and more money. He decided to sign the contract, and, with López, he began preparing for the match against Luis Henrique in Orlando, Florida.

FRANCIS NGANNOU

Ngannou vs. UFC

The UFC is the world's foremost MMA promotional company, hosting televised events that broadcast globally. With the UFC's international set of fighters, people across the world are interested in watching. The UFC divides its fights into various divisions based on fighters' weights. Ngannou was placed into the heavyweight division, in which fighters weigh a minimum of 206 lbs.

Events also fall into different categories depending on how they are aired. Numbered events, such as UFC 218, are pay-per-view, while other events (such as UFC on Fox) air on specific television channels.

Ngannou's first UFC fight, against Luis Henrique of Brazil, took place on December 9, 2015. It was an impressive **debut** for Ngannou in which, for the first time, he had a chance to demonstrate his immense punching power to a wide audience. In round one of the fight, Ngannou started off with some successful leg kicks. Although Henrique managed to trip Ngannou with a leg kick of his own, Ngannou was eventually able to regain his footing. They spent the rest of the round **clinching**, their arms wrapped around each other in a hold. In the second round, Henrique tried to close the distance to avoid any more kicks from Ngannou. However, Ngan-

Ngannou hits Henrique with a devastating punch.

nou rained down strikes on Henrique, and he backed his opponent into a corner. Finally, Ngannou landed a left **uppercut** that brought Henrique down.

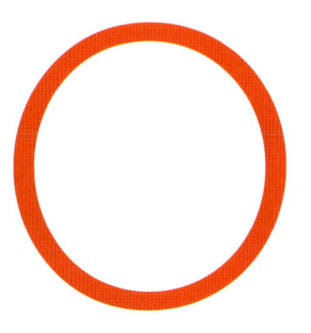

One MMA analyst described Ngannou's fight as "one of the most vicious heavyweight **knockouts** in recent history." The UFC was impressed as well. "SERIOUS POWER!!!," they said on Twitter. "Welcome to the UFC @Francis_Ngannou!"

That was only the beginning. From 2015 to 2017, Ngannou continued winning one fight after the next, often in just the first round. He took on the nickname "The Predator." He shattered the winning streaks of numerous opponents who had been fighting much longer than him. For example, Bojan Mihajlovic had a ten-win streak when Ngannou fought him in the ring. However, when Ngannou landed a left-handed strike to the face, Mihajlovic was knocked to the ground. Mihajlovic was unable to withstand the **ground-and-pound** that followed, and Ngannou won in the first round by stoppage.

As Ngannou accumulated a six-fight UFC winning streak, people in the MMA world really started to notice him. One commentator wrote, "In more than 25 years of following mixed martial arts, Francis Ngannou is the scariest puncher I've ever seen." The president of the UFC himself, Dana White, said that he was anticipating great things from Ngannou. "I like Francis Ngannou," White said. "I think he's going to be the next big thing, both literally and figuratively."

People in Cameroon were noticing too. While only a few Cameroonians followed Ngannou's early MMA fights, people were now starting to call him, asking, "Was that you on TV?" Some fans told him stories of how they started to believe their own dreams were possible once they saw him fighting on TV. More and more, Cameroonians tuned into Ngannou's fights, even though it

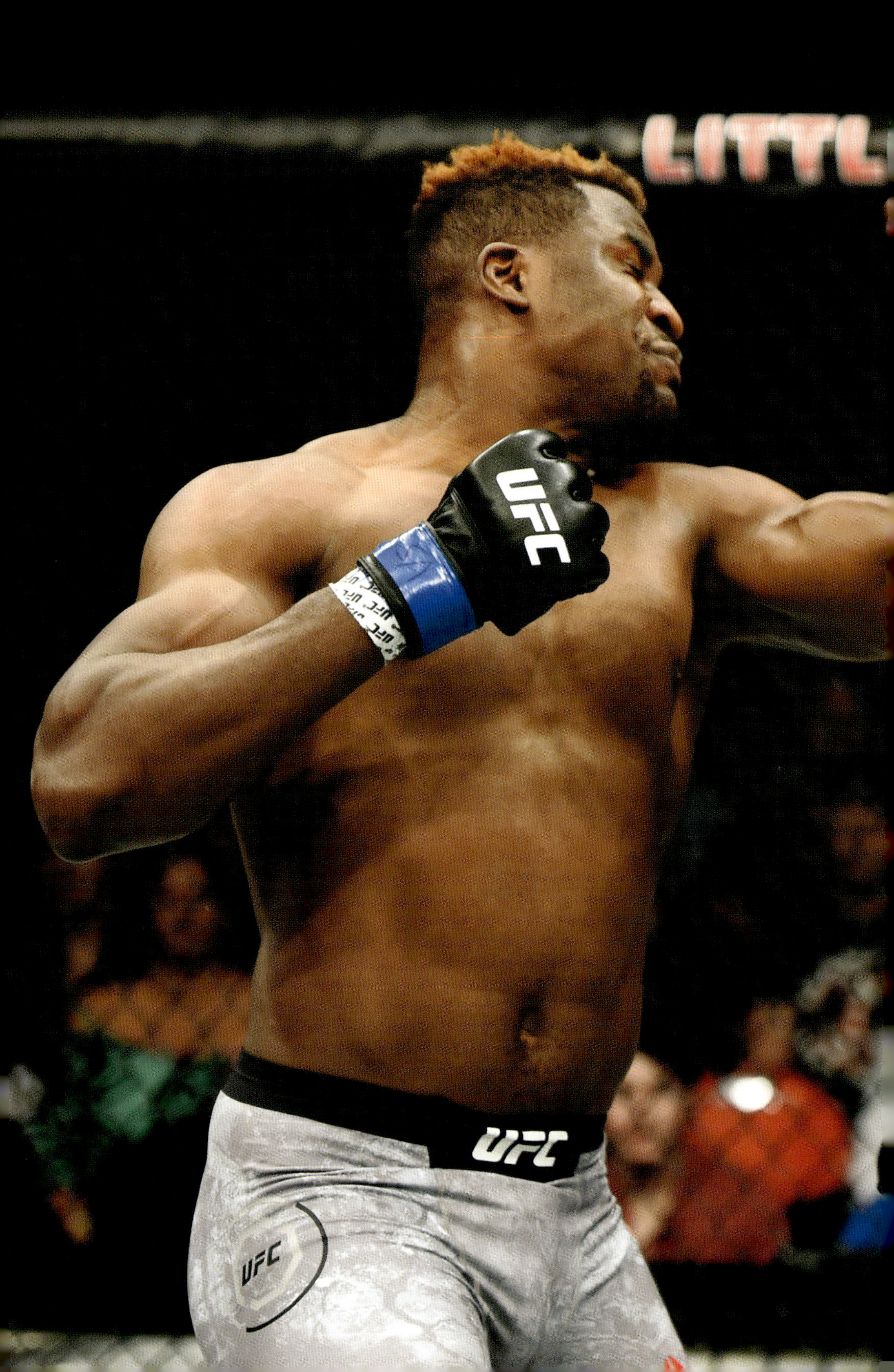
UFC
UFC
UFC

'He's the Man'

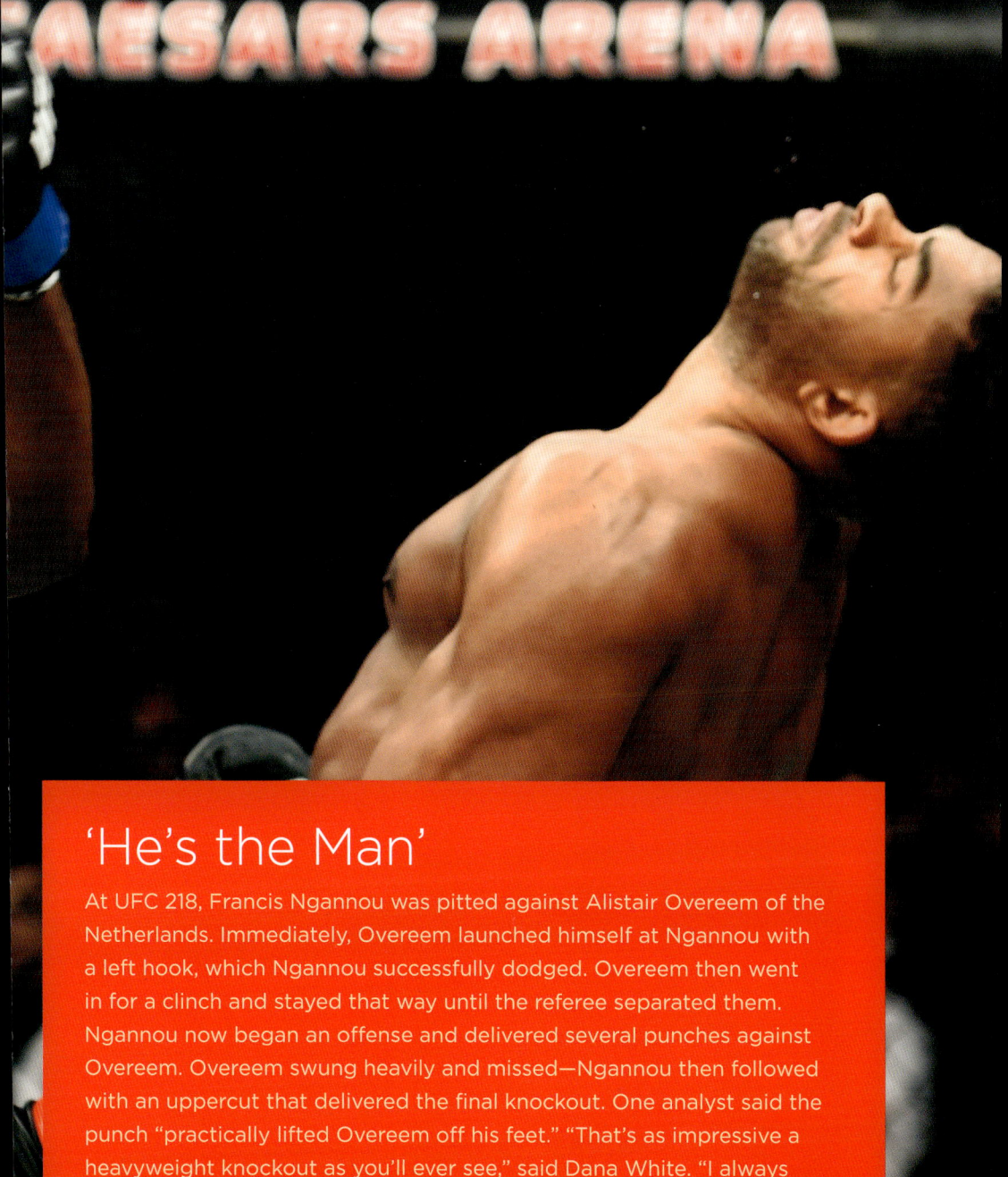

At UFC 218, Francis Ngannou was pitted against Alistair Overeem of the Netherlands. Immediately, Overeem launched himself at Ngannou with a left hook, which Ngannou successfully dodged. Overeem then went in for a clinch and stayed that way until the referee separated them. Ngannou now began an offense and delivered several punches against Overeem. Overeem swung heavily and missed—Ngannou then followed with an uppercut that delivered the final knockout. One analyst said the punch "practically lifted Overeem off his feet." "That's as impressive a heavyweight knockout as you'll ever see," said Dana White. "I always believed in this guy since I met him. I thought he was going to be the man, and, boy, did he look like the man tonight."

sometimes meant waking up early in the morning because of the time difference.

In all, Ngannou's winning streak included Luis Henrique, Curtis Blaydes, Bojan Mihajlovic, Anthony Hamilton, Andrei Arlovski, and Alistair Overeem.

Then came Ngannou's biggest UFC challenge yet — a fight for the title against heavyweight champion Stipe Miocic. It was not an easy fight to predict. While Miocic had a higher striking rate than Ngannou, Ngannou had a higher **knockdown** rate. Miocic was a better wrestler, but Ngannou had stopped 75 percent of all **takedowns** during his UFC career. The fight could go either way.

The match went on for a full five minutes, lasting five rounds. Ngannou had never gone that long in a fight before—he was accustomed to first- and second-round knockouts. Unfortunately, Miocic won by unanimous decision after the judges tallied up the points. He kept his championship title, and Ngannou's winning streak came to an end.

The loss was a big disappointment for Ngannou. Then, at his next UFC fight that July, he lost by decision again, this time against Derrick Lewis. It became clear that Ngannou was doing something wrong.

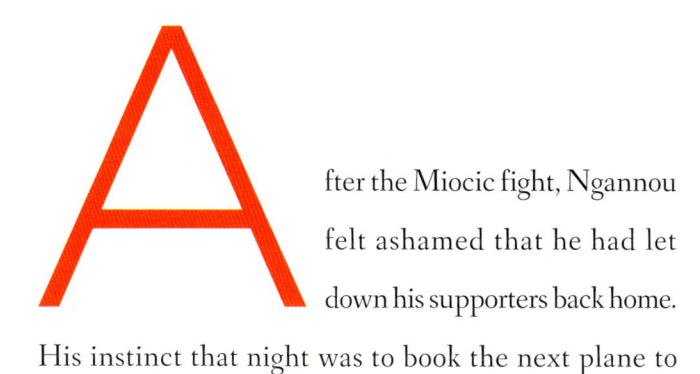

After the Miocic fight, Ngannou felt ashamed that he had let down his supporters back home. His instinct that night was to book the next plane to

A Cameroonian fan holds a poster of Ngannou.

Cameroon, as he wanted some time in his home country. Still, the shame followed him. "I didn't even want people to recognize me," he remembers.

However, to his surprise, people cheered and congratulated him everywhere he went. They told him how proud they were that a Cameroonian had reached such a level of worldwide recognition. They didn't care that he lost.

That was when he really started to understand that the people of Cameroon would support him no matter what. They loved seeing him up on the screen in front of the world, and he made them proud. "My strength was Cameroon now," Ngannou recalls. "They're the only people that didn't care [about me losing]. So now I'm like, 'Okay, let's make them happy.'"

In the wake of his losses, Ngannou took time to reflect on how he could improve. When he rewatched the Miocic fight, he recognized he was thinking too much about trying to knock his opponent out, and that was causing him to rush. In other words, Ngannou cared excessively about winning during his fights, and he was too concerned with what other people would think if he lost. Back when he started MMA, however, he wasn't focused on winning or losing. He did MMA because it was fun! That was what he needed to get back to. He would just do his best, enjoy the fight, and forget everything else.

After gaining these important insights, Ngannou started to win again. Against Curtis Blaydes, he won by knockout in just 45 seconds. Against Cain Velasquez, he won in a mere 26 seconds. He defeated Junior Dos Santos and Jairzinho Rozenstruik with knockouts as well. The Predator was back—and he was a force to be reckoned with.

Then came the big test: a rematch with Miocic. Both fighters had learned a lot in the three years since their last fight, and now Ngannou had a chance for a comeback. He was motivated by the thought of crowds across Cameroon staying up late into the night to watch the fight. Ngannou's mother would be among them.

The fight took place at UFC 260 on March 27, 2021. It was a triumph! In the second round, Ngannou struck Miocic with an uppercut that knocked him out. As a result, Ngannou won the heavyweight championship. Videos circulated

Ngannou vs. Miocic, 2021

on the Internet of Cameroonians celebrating, thrilled to be of the same nation as Ngannou. After the win, Ngannou toured Cameroon, greeting flocks of fans and holding his championship belt up for everyone to see. It was a special moment in Ngannou's life and career as an MMA fighter.

For two years after winning the heavyweight title against Miocic, Ngannou defended the title. Unfortunately, during that same time the relationship between Ngannou and the UFC began to sour. Ngannou felt that his contract with the UFC constrained him too much. For example, he wanted to participate in boxing matches outside of the UFC, but under his contract he was not permitted to do so. In addition, he did not feel that fighters received sufficient pay for their fights.

Ngannou negotiated with the UFC for a long time to make adjustments to the contract. He requested that the UFC provide health insurance for all fighters. He also asked that the UFC allow personal sponsorships during fights, which would permit individual fighters to form partnerships with brands for money. The UFC did not accommodate these demands, although they did offer to increase Ngannou's pay. White said that the final deal would have made Francis Ngannou the highest-earning UFC heavyweight ever. Still, Ngannou did not want to make **concessions** regarding what he could and could not do. "This is very important, dignity and freedom," he stated. "I need freedom and to control my destiny, not have people control it for me."

After many months of negotiations, Ngannou turned down the UFC's offer. The UFC released Ngannou from his contract, and in January 2023, Ngannou left the organization. White stripped him of his championship title.

With the UFC behind him, Ngannou had his mind set again on boxing. Later in 2023, he struck a deal with the Professional Fighters League (PFL), an MMA organization and a competitor of the UFC.

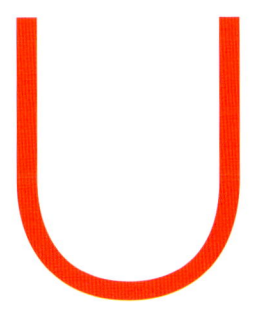

Under the contract, Ngannou must fight MMA exclusively on PFL's broadcasting network. However, he is free to fight in boxing matches outside the PFL as well.

Because Ngannou speaks strongly for fighters' rights, he also negotiated on behalf of other PFL fighters. For example, he included a $2 million guarantee to all of his future opponents, meaning that anyone who fought him would be guaranteed a minimum payout of $2 million. Additionally,

Ngannou finally got the chance to box in 2023.

the PFL made Ngannou the chairman of its Africa division, with the goal of expanding MMA into that continent. Ngannou announced that he believed the organization would provide "great African fighters the opportunity to compete on a global platform." Ngannou was showing that he was not just a good fighter but also a strong businessman.

Ngannou continued fighting in the boxing ring as he always desired. His first boxing match, against Tyson Fury, took place in Saudi Arabia. It was a special fight—for his past UFC fights in the U.S., Ngannou had been unsuccessful at acquiring **visas** for his family so they could travel to see him. At the fight against Tyson Fury, however, they made it. His mother and siblings were in the audience, watching him in person for the first time. His family had always been an important part of his life, and Ngannou was proud to have them watch his dream become a reality.

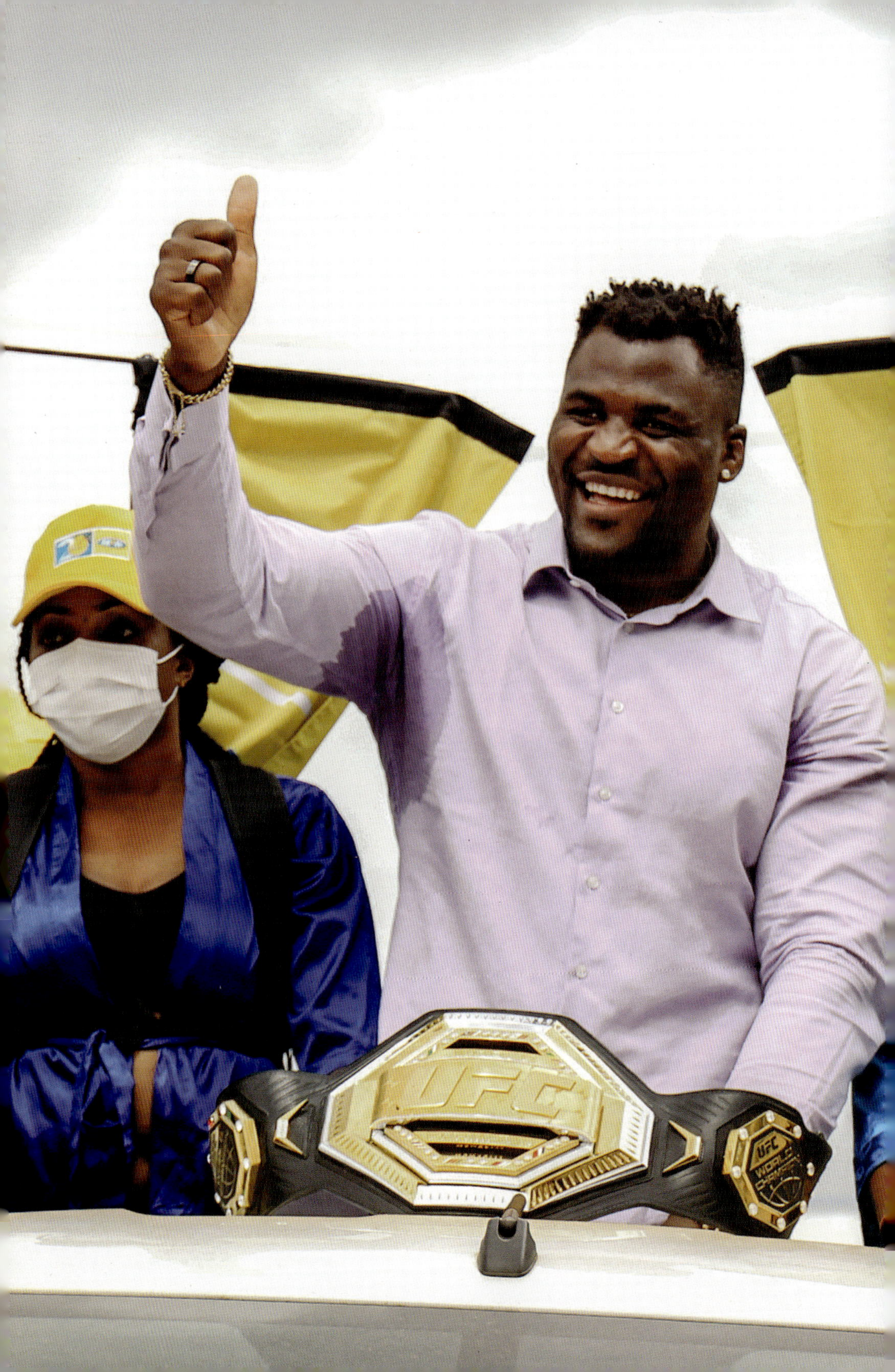
UFC

FRANCIS NGANNOU

Reflections

Ngannou holds a strong set of values that have been influenced by the events and people of his life. He cherishes his family, believes in the importance of constant self-improvement, donates to Cameroon, and speaks frequently about the hard life of African migrants.

OPPOSITE: Francis Ngannou holds his championship belt, as he rides in a truck through the streets of Bafoussam, Cameroon, on May 1, 2021.

Despite the uncertainty he experienced growing up, Ngannou maintained a strong connection with his family. "We were very bound, very, very close," he says. The family always made sure to take care of one another. When he had to go to the hospital, for example, everybody in the family contributed to help pay for the bills. "So, it wasn't my money, your money—it was ours," he says. "You see them around you, guarding, doing everything to support you in that position [when] you are the most vulnerable."

It was that close-knit relationship that made Ngannou want to provide a better life not just for himself but for all his family. As he acquired money from professional fighting, he always made sure to send money home. Today, he is very happy that money is no longer a major concern for his family.

Ngannou wanted to be a boxer, but his coaches convinced him that he would find more success in MMA.

Despite his many MMA wins, Ngannou is aware that his skills will always require improvement. He was often aware that he had less experience than his opponents, and he trained hard to make up for it. "I'm in the sport to learn," he says. In particular, he remembers that his first fight against Miocic taught him a lot about combat and MMA. At the post-fight press conference, he said, "Tonight I learned more than I have learned in the past four years in this game." He realized the hard truth that sometimes the only way to learn is to fail. He therefore believes that you should never think you are as good as you can be—you can always get better. "If you stay comfortable with something, that's the day that you start to lose it," says Ngannou.

Because Ngannou spent so much time as a migrant, he also speaks out in defense of the migrants who continue to cross from Africa into Europe. They still experience the same hardships he did. For example, in June 2022, more than 23 people died at the border between Spain and Morocco. The Moroccan Association for Human Rights suggests that the deaths happened after authorities used smoke bombs and tear gas on a large crowd of migrants approaching the fences. "I couldn't sleep for two days," Ngannou told the press after seeing the video. But he found the experience common. "It's some of the most barbaric, inhumane treatment you could ever imagine... Yes, it's illegal [to cross borders without permission], but it's our only way out."

Ngannou often shares his own story as a migrant from Cameroon and the extreme adversity he endured. For example, to cross from Niger into Algeria, he rode in the bed of a smuggler's truck, tightly packed with other migrants. He found himself at the edge of the truck, holding on to keep from falling out. As the hours on the road passed, he got cramps. But he couldn't let go. If he fell, he would be left on his own in the searing days and freezing nights of the Sahara Desert. "They [the smugglers] won't stop," Ngannou recalls. "Letting go is like letting your life go."

Ngannou remembers that, in Morocco, he had only a blanket and a plastic tarp to protect his few belongings from the rain. He sought different ways of escaping into Spain. First, he tried crossing the six-meter fences that separated Morocco from two Spanish **enclaves** called Ceuta and Melilla. These borders were heavily guarded, however, and he got cut badly on the barbed wire. Every time he failed at crossing, he was arrested by Moroccan police and expelled from the country. And every time

The Moroccan border with Ceuta

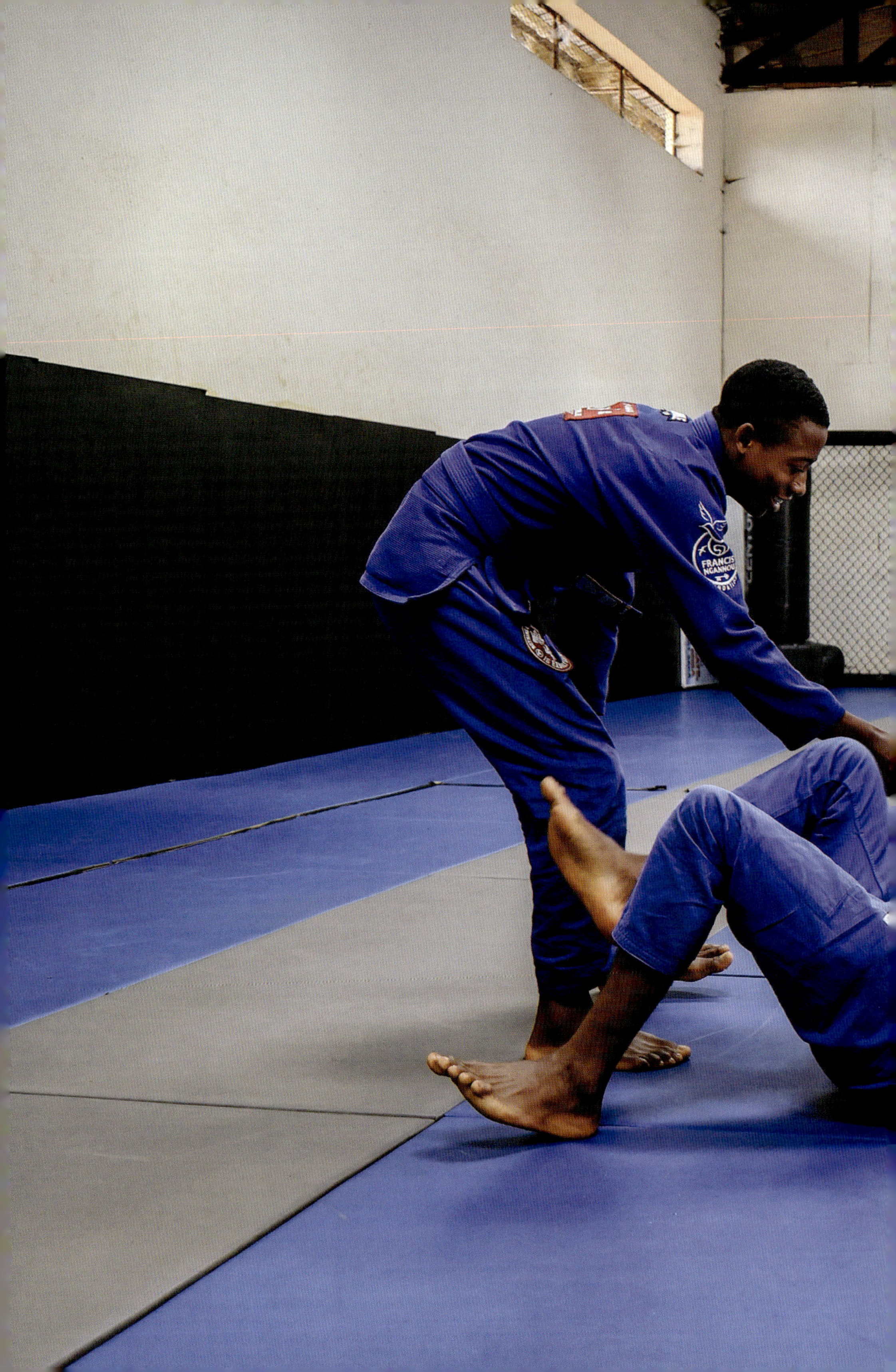
FRANCIS

The Francis Ngannou Foundation

Francis Ngannou believes in the importance of giving back through **philanthropy**. In 2018, he started the Francis Ngannou Foundation to support underserved children and schools in Cameroon. He founded Cameroon's first MMA gym to give Cameroonian children more opportunities to pursue their dreams. He doesn't want them to have the same experience he did when he was a child, when there were few opportunities to pursue the sport of fighting in Cameroon. The foundation has also provided computer labs, school materials, Covid-19 supplies, and many school renovations to the people of Cameroon.

he was made to leave, he trekked back to the border to try again.

When he realized crossing the fences was futile, he began teaming up with other migrants to cross by sea. Although he failed numerous times, he gained enough experience that people started asking him to captain their boats. His nickname in Tangier became "Van Damme," after the Belgian fighter and actor.

For each ocean attempt, he would pool money with other migrants to buy an inflatable raft. This raft could typically hold around ten people. They got life vests for themselves or made makeshift ones from the inner tubes of tires. Then they would check the forecast to see when the sea would be calm. The day of the journey, they would set off early in the morning, when police **vigilance** was low. They had to time their entry into the water to avoid large waves that could slam their raft into the rocks and wreck it. Once at sea, they hoped to reach Spanish waters by paddling. They could then call the Spanish Red Cross and be rescued.

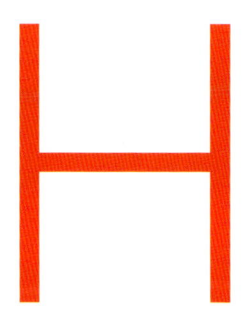

He made six failed attempts by ocean—it was only on the seventh attempt that he finally succeeded. Many people make it across, he notes, but there are many other migrants who have died trying. Ngannou hopes to bring greater awareness of their treacherous paths to Europe and their desperation for a better life.

Ngannou sometimes thinks about all that he has been through and how, during much of his life, he wondered why he and his family had to suffer. He says he would never wish for anyone to go through what he did. At the same time, he believes that, in a way, his hard past was also a blessing.

"It seems that my journey was just preparing me for this moment, for the life that I'm having now," he says. "I'm not afraid of falling because I know that I have the ability to stand up. And that's what my life taught me." The power to persevere got him out of Cameroon, into Europe, and up the rankings of the UFC. By remembering that he can achieve anything he sets his mind to, he knows that there is nothing he cannot overcome.

Francis Ngannou reacts after his heavyweight championship fight against Ciryl Gane at UFC 270 on January 22, 2022 in Anaheim, California.

Selected Bibliography

Dundas, Chad. "From Homeless to UFC's Next Big Thing: Francis Ngannou's Amazing Journey." *Bleacher Report*, December 1, 2017. https://bleacherreport.com/articles/2746156-from-homeless-to-ufcs-next-big-thing-francis-ngannous-amazing-journey.

Keown, Tim. "Francis Ngannou's Miraculous Journey." *ESPN, ESPN Enterprises*, January 21, 2022. https://www.espn.com/espn/feature/story/_/id/33100543/francis-ngannou-miraculous-journey-ufc-stardom.

Mann, Richard. "UFC 220: Stipe Miocic vs. Francis Ngannou statistical breakdown." *ESPN, ESPN Enterprises*, January 17, 2018. https://www.espn.com/mma/story/_/id/22131777/ufc-220-stipe-miocic-vs-francis-ngannou-breaking-striking-power-wrestling-abilities-stat-stat.

Martinez, A. "How Francis Ngannou made it from the sand mines of Cameroon to an MMA championship." *NPR*, June 29, 2023. https://www.npr.org/2023/06/29/1184976836/how-francis-ngannou-made-it-from-the-sand-mines-of-cameroon-to-an-mma-championsh.

Okamoto, Brett. "Inside the negotiations that brought the No. 1 heavyweight in the world, Francis Ngannou, to the PFL." *ESPN, ESPN Enterprises*, May 23, 2023. https://www.espn.com/mma/story/_/id/37702902/why-francis-ngannou-left-ufc-signed-pfl-contract-deal.

Rogan, Joe, host. "JRE MMA Show #99 with Francis Ngannou." *The Joe Rogan Experience,* February 2021. https://open.spotify.com/episode/6h2N6q4gUZ32z1IsvyXFKh?si=3eb6cad93f2e40ed.

Tyson, Mike, host. "Francis Ngannou | Hotboxin' with Mike Tyson." *YouTube*, uploaded by Mike Tyson, May 1, 2020. www.youtube.com/watch?v=NlIWOM4bOSk.

Glossary

clinch — a hold when two fighters move in close and wrap their arms around each other

concession — a thing yielded or given

debut — a first public performance

enclave — a territory surrounded by a foreign territory

ground-and-pound — the process of straddling an opponent on the mat and delivering multiple punches

heavyweight — a fighter who weighs 206–265 pounds (93.4–120.2 kg)

knockdown — what occurs when a fighter is knocked to the mat but is able to get back up

knockout — what occurs when a fighter is knocked to the mat, cannot get back up, and loses a fight

migrant — a person who leaves their home country in search of a better life

ominous — threatening

philanthropy — the act of donating and promoting human welfare

regimen — a regular course of exercise and/or diet to promote health

repatriation — the return of a person to their home country

shoulder lock — a hold that makes it difficult or painful for an opponent to move their shoulder

submission	the act of securing a hold on an opponent that causes the opponent to tap out as a result of the pain and discomfort
takedown	the act of pulling an opponent to the ground to gain an advantage
tap out	to signal defeat by tapping on the floor or on a part of the opponent's body
uppercut	a strike that connects with the opponent's chin from below
vigilance	close watch
visa	permission from a government to enter or exit a country

Websites

Francis Ngannou Foundation
https://francisngannoufoundation.com
Explore how Francis Ngannou has given back to Cameroon through the Francis Ngannou Foundation.

Francis Ngannou (Heavyweight) MMA Profile – ESPN
https://www.espn.com/mma/fighter/_/id/3933168/francisngannou
Read up on Francis Ngannou's stats and compare him to other MMA fighters.

JRE MMA Show #99 with Francis Ngannou
https://open.spotify.com/episode/6h2N6q4gUZ32z1lsvyXFKh?si=3eb6cad93f2e40ed
In this podcast, Francis Ngannou vividly describes his experience growing up in Cameroon, crossing into Europe, and learning MMA.

Ngannou Documentary Series
https://www.youtube.com/playlist?list=PLz_xb_BPOO8Rh3S6sksndmq1MZSCW6QX0
This documentary tells the story of Francis Ngannou's life, from Cameroon to Paris to MMA fighting.

Index

Arlovski, Andrei, 50
Batié, 15, 17, 22, 32
Benzina, Rachid, 40
Blaydes, Curtis, 50, 54
boxing, 13, 17, 25, 27, 31, 35, 36, 37, 38, 40, 41, 57, 58, 59, 61
Cameroon, 9, 13, 15, 16, 22, 25, 26, 27, 28, 29, 37, 39, 47, 53, 55, 57, 63, 67, 71, 74
Carmont, Didier, 35, 36, 37, 38,
Ceuta, 68, 69
Dos Santos, Junior, 54
Douala, 25, 26
Fosso, Emmanuel, 15, 20
Francis Ngannou Foundation, 71
Fury, Tyson, 61
Hamilton, Anthony, 50
heavyweight, 10, 42, 45, 49, 50, 55, 57, 58
López, Fernand, 37, 38, 40, 41
Henrique, Luis, 41, 43, 44, 45, 50
Melilla, 68
Mihajlovic, Bojan, 46, 50
Miocic, Stipe, 50, 51, 53, 55, 56, 57, 66
mixed martial arts (MMA), 10, 13, 31, 36, 37, 38, 40, 41, 42, 45, 46, 47, 54, 57, 59, 61, 66, 71
MMA Factory, 37, 38
Morocco, 27, 67, 68
Christine, Kamegni, 15
Overeem, Alistair, 49, 50
Paris, 15, 32
poverty, 13, 17
Professional Fighters League (PFL), 59, 61
Rozenstruik, Jairzinho, 54
Spain, 28, 29, 67, 68
The Predator, 46, 54
Tyson, Mike, 17, 19, 28
Ultimate Fighting Championship (UFC), 10, 37, 41, 42, 43, 45, 46, 49, 50, 51, 55, 57, 58, 59, 61, 74
United States, 39
Van Damme, 72
Velasquez, Cain, 54
White, Dana, 46, 47, 49, 58

80